TARGETED BY WORK BULLIES

Stories from Hell

Gloria Moraga

This book is dedicated to all workers who feel bullied.

Copyright © 2019 by Gloria Moraga. All Right Reserved.

No part of this publication may be reproduced, distributed, or transmitted in any form or by any means, including photocopying, recording, or other electronic or mechanical methods, or by any information storage and retrieval system without the prior written permission of the publisher, except in the case of very brief quotations embodied in critical reviews and certain other noncommercial uses permitted by copyright law.

CONTENTS

Title Page	1
Dedication	3
Copyright	4
Forward	7
Part One – The Problem	11
Bullies Are Everywhere	13
Chapter One	14
What is a Work Bully?	15
Chapter Two	19
Targeted by Bullies	20
Chapter Three	23
The University Bullies	24
Chapter Four	27
The Numbers	28
Part Two	33
Our Stories	35
Chapter Five	36
Laura's Story	37
Chapter Six	43
Gloria's Story	44
Chapter Seven	53

Anthony's Story	54
Chapter Eight	61
Pearl's Story	62
Chapter Nine	67
Carol's Story	68
Part Three	73
How to Stop work Bullies	75
Chapter Ten	76
Let's Stop Them	77
Chapter Eleven	79
The Healthy Workplace Bill	80
Chapter Twelve	82
This is Worth Repeating	83
Chapter Thirteen	85
Let's Beat the Bullies	86
Acknowledgments	89
Call to Action	91

FORWARD

"There's People In Hell Who Want Ice Water..."

NELSON ALGREN, "THE MAN WITH THE GOLDEN ARM"

It happened every radio shift. I worked 10 p.m. to 8 a.m. and every time I paused or mispronounced a word; or if I was two seconds late rolling a tape; the phone in the control room would begin to blink. The phone didn't make a sound, but the red light would blink." Blink. Blink. Blink. I would pick up the receiver as soon as possible, usually once the newsman in the next room would begin his report. And then the screaming would begin.

Gloria Moraga, My First Boss-Bully, 1974

I began researching workplace bullying for my Podcast, *"One-On-One - Communications in the Digital Age."* I was producing a series of reports on communication difficulties at work. I called the Series *"Wanting Ice Water..."* for the wonderful quote from Nelson Algren's, *"The Man With the Golden Arm."* A graphic story about addiction and heroin withdrawal. I liked the quote because I had been targeted in my job by two workplace bullies; and I felt like I was in hell most of the time.

I produced two podcast episodes on workplace bullying.

I moved on to other issues; but the workplace bullying topic haunts me. I was stunned when I read the statistics from the **Workplace Bullying Institute**. My next shock was the fact that the United States has failed to pass legislation protecting American workers from bullying supervisors and colleagues.

What the hell is the matter with us? We are the only Western nation that does not provide legal protection for workers from bullies. Disgraceful.

As I researched, my notes began to fill one of my portable hard drives. So, here I am. And I hope you are there; reading and listening to the stories from the "Targets" of workplace bullies.

This short book is written in three parts, the problem, the personal stories, and possible solutions. Part three is short, I'm ashamed to say. U.S. legal protection for workers is pitiful.

As a former political reporter, I believe in the legislative process, no matter how messy it may be. Lawmakers work for us. We need workplace protection from bullies. Yet, I also know how difficult it is to get action from the legislature. Look at where we are with Gun Control or Health Care Reform or Climate Change.

All change for the better must begin with us.

Just like mopping the floor or cleaning the litter box, if we don't do it, it's not going to get done.

I am not an attorney and never played one on television, still I've searched for concrete, real-life suggestions on how you can deal with your bullies. But without legal protections we really do not have many options.

It is extremely difficult to offer advice when even the experts admit that the problem – the bullying – might get worse if you complain.

Please keep that in mind as you read and listen. Bottom line, like me and so many others sometimes the only solution is to leave the job you love.

Because our laws are weak, and solutions are weaker; I thought about leaving this topic behind, I could update it when some brave legislator decided to do something. No. I couldn't wait. I need to tell my story and my number one goal is to let you know you are not alone. There are millions of us who feel bullied and if you are feeling bullied at work you most likely are being bullied.

I wrote this to help exorcise some of my demons. Yup, the bullies still haunt me. It hurts to think about the bullying. I know you hurt too. And we all need to reach out to each other to fight these people.

My love of movies and books has helped me survive. I am a film fanatic, so I've included quotes from some of my favorite movies and books that relate to the stories I am sharing.

So, let's begin.

PART ONE – THE PROBLEM

BULLIES ARE EVERYWHERE

"Thirty million American workers have been or are now being bullied at work. Another 30 million have witnessed it. These proportions are epidemic-level."

The Workplace Bullying Institute

CHAPTER ONE

WHAT IS A WORK BULLY?

"I would rather be a little nobody, then to be an evil somebody."

Abraham Lincoln

Bullies at work are a fact of life. Bullies aren't just children any more tormenting other little ones on the playground. They are in the workforce, they are powerful, and they are pervasive.

Here are some of the definitions of Bullying.

This is from the "*Merriam-Webster*" online dictionary.

Bully (noun)

bul·ly | \ ˈbu̇-lē , ˈbə-\ *plural* **bullies** a blustering, **browbeating** person; especially: one who is habitually cruel, insulting, or threatening to others who are weaker, smaller, or in some way vulnerable.

Bully (verb) bullied; bullying
transitive verb

    1. to treat (someone) in a cruel, insulting, threatening, or aggressive fashion.

    2. to cause (someone) to do something by means of force or coercion.

    3. to use language or behavior that is cruel, insulting, threatening, or aggressive.

That is *"Webster's"* definition.

This is from the *"Healthy Workplace Bill"*:

"Workplace Bullying is repeated, health-harming mistreatment of one or more persons (the **targets**) by one or more perpetrators: abusive conduct that takes one or more of the following forms:

- Verbal abuse, or
- Threatening, intimidating or humiliating behaviors (including nonverbal), or
- Work interference – sabotage – which prevents work from getting done, or
- Some combination of one or more.

And finally, this is from the **Workplace Bullying Institute's** *"2017 Workplace Bullying Survey,"*

"We used the definition of workplace bullying that matches perfectly the definition codified in the *"Healthy Workplace Bill."* Bullying is repeated mistreatment but also "abusive conduct."

In the United States bullies are more powerful that workers. But there is some hope.

There is a **Workplace Bullying Institute** and a *"Healthy Workplace Bill"* and a **National Campaign** to make workplace bullying illegal. I will be quoting statistics from these organizations in this book. It's important because Workplace Bullying is not currently illegal.

I am not an attorney, a doctor or a psychologist; I'm not working on my doctoral dissertation on the psychology of Workplace Bullying. I am a former Target of a bully. I was harassed, given impossible assignments, denied the tools I needed to do my job properly and more.

The bullying took a toll on my health and my family. I developed stomach problems, suffered from depression. I couldn't sleep; I overate, I gained weight.

I saw a doctor and a psychiatrist and a therapist. I was told I was fine because I got up and went to work each day, the bullying and depression were not affecting my ability to continue to be a working, wage-earner. "It's not that bad," the doctors said. I got a prescription for sleeping pills and antidepressants.

The bullying continued. I seemed fine on the outside. And on the inside? I was a mess.

I survived. I am a survivor.

I am also a communicator, an educated, strong, successful woman who suffered through years of bullying in my public relations job at a local university.

Once I was targeted by the bullies I moved through these stages.

I was shocked, I couldn't believe anybody would target me, I was the most experienced person in the office. I worked 24 – seven. I was confused, sad and dismayed, why is this happening to me? I didn't deserve this. I was embarrassed and ashamed. They wanted to fire me. I felt worthless and expendable. I didn't want anyone to know what they were doing to me. Yet everyone knew. I saw pity in my coworker's eyes. Colleagues began avoiding me. They were too busy for lunch. I felt like it was my fault.

I began looking for another job. We were in a recession. I was too old. I was disabled. I was washed up. I had no friends. I felt sick and alone.

My bullying and my reaction to being bullied are not unique. I now know other workers feel the same way. I was shocked when I realized I was not alone.

When I read the findings in the **Workplace Bullying Institute's**, *"2017 U.S. Workplace Bullying Survey,"* a light turned on in my brain. "Oh my gosh!" I thought. It's happening everywhere!

That 2017 survey included this question for the first time, "At work, what has been your personal experience with the following types of repeated mistreatment: abusive conduct that is threatening, intimidating, humiliating, work sabotage or verbal abuse?"

That question helped the experts come up with the "60 Million Workers" statistic!

Not only are workers being bullied in epidemic proportions: but coworkers are seeing it.

What a nightmare. I included the definitions of workplace bullying from the experts because I want to make sure we are all on the same page. I want to make sure you do not doubt yourself.

Do you see your bully in the definitions and descriptions? If any of them apply to you then you are being bullied.

Sometimes we just need someone from outside our situation to give us validation.

On the other hand, some of us who have been bullied at work don't need to look up the definition. We are living it every day. And it is, as I said, a nightmare.

CHAPTER TWO

TARGETED BY BULLIES

"If you are being bullied, you are a target. It's not your fault, the bully targets you!"

The Workplace Bullying Institute

The Washington D.C. Bully

My bureau chief never liked me. I sometimes wonder how different my professional life would have been if he would have mentored me or just tried to accept me. But he did not.

I think he resented the fact that his boss wanted him to hire me; and so, he did. He bullied me as much as he could. Once he assigned me to go to the State Department and find a woman by the name of Lil Grub and interview her.

What? Was all I could manage.

That was the assignment. A woman by the name of Lil Grub was in Washington to speak with someone at the State Department about her nephew who was a missionary in some foreign country. The bureau's station in Ohio wanted an interview. Never mind that they could have interviewed Lil Grub before she boarded the plan for D.C. No. That would have been too easy.

So off we went to the State Department. Me and my photographer David Chase. I complained all the way there. Poor David. How are we going to find her? The State Department is huge. They are going to laugh at us. Security is really tight there. They are not going to let us wander around looking for some woman from Dayton, Ohio.

We found her. We found her because I was nice to the security personnel. They helped us. The bureau chief was disappointed.

After five years at the Bureau I became an accepted annoyance to this bully. That was when I fell in a parking garage and broke my leg. I was on the job. It was a dark hallway, in a building next to CBS News. The stairs were not marked. It was a bad break.

When I returned to work; my leg was still healing, and I was in a lot of pain. One of my assignments was to sit in the federal courthouse for the Oliver North trial. I was taking notes and covering the trial; the problem was sitting for a long time was very painful. My doctor wrote a note that said, I can walk, I can work, I can report, I just can't sit for eight hours a day.

I was called in to the bureau chief's office on the Monday morning after I shared the doctor's note with him. He and the assistant bureau chief were in the office and they asked me to close the door.

I was being fired. They said they had hoped that the court assignment would help me readjust to returning to work. But since I can't sit for long periods, there was no longer a place for me in the bureau. Sorry. They tried to accommodate my disability, but they had to hire an able-bodied correspondent.

I asked then to please send me their decision in an e-mail and I left without a word. I cried all the way home. One week later I received the e-mail and my termination information.

I called a civil rights attorney. We sued. Using the *"American's with*

Disabilities Act", which requires reasonable workplace accommodations. I got my job back. It was all I wanted. I should have sued for damages and retired; but I had hope then.

That hope was beaten out of me when I went to work for the university bullies.

CHAPTER THREE

THE UNIVERSITY BULLIES

"The reason that University politics is so vicious is because the stakes are so small."

Henry Kissinger

I really loved my job and I love working. I was a workaholic but in a good way. I enjoyed throwing myself into my stories and projects. My passion made me a better television reporter, a good news manager, and a popular university public relations supervisor.

I earned my master's degree when I was in Washington, D.C. working full time. I attended classes at The American University on Saturday's for two years. That degree, in print Journalism and Public Affairs meant a lot to me. My bullies hated me for it.

Bottom line they did not have advanced degrees. And it made them feel insecure. Because after all, this was a college campus and we were surrounded by people with Ph.D.'s.

The bullying I suffered through at the state college was painful and demoralizing. I had worked my way up to an associate vice president's position, when the bullies took over, they systematically removed every form of support. I was demoted without cause, moved to a small storage room, given computers and equipment that malfunctioned. And I was assigned tasks that needed a team of people to complete.

I never shot video in my career; but I was assigned to shoot and edit video. I learned quickly, and was good. I was assigned the task of producing seven television shows. My duties included shooting all the video, booking guests, editing videos, writing all the scripts, writing text for the web sites, editing all post-production videos.

I won awards. Still the bullying never stopped. I was demoted again and again.

Being the target of the bullies at my workplace sapped some of my passion; and I was lost without it. It changed me. I became a different person. A person I didn't like very much. I lost touch with friends. I was afraid to talk about it. I didn't want my family to know. I felt ashamed. I felt broken. I lost confidence. I was afraid.

I was also physically ill. I developed a raging ulcer. I stopped sleeping more than a couple of hours each night.

And it's taken me more than two years to recover mentally. Antibiotics helped the ulcer calm down, but it'll always be there, ready to flare up. The psychological scars remain.

Here are the questions I've asked myself a million times, "Did I **let** them do it? Was it my fault for not fighting back a little more? Am I to blame?"

The answer, of course, is, "No!" We are not going there. It was not my fault and it is not yours. No way!

It's the bully who is at fault. It's the person who enjoys tormenting someone a little more vulnerable, a little less strong. Blame them! And fight them.

This book is my way of letting all of you know that you are not alone. When you are being bullied at work you feel isolated and tormented and alone. That's what they want. I'm here to say you are not alone and there are steps you can take so survive and thrive.

Because there is Life after the Bully!

CHAPTER FOUR

THE NUMBERS

*If You Are Being Bullied at
Work You Are Not Alone*

From the WBI 2017 U.S. Workplace Bullying Survey

It's a Crisis – It's an Epidemic
It's Got to Stop!

"Some people try to be tall by cutting off the heads of others."

Paramahansa Yogananda

The stories in this book are real. Every example of bullying really happened. The stories in Part Two are just short examples of what happened to former co-workers, family and friends who lived through their bullying boss or bullying colleagues to tell their story. I am changing names and places and some situations.

I'm doing it to protect the people I'm writing about and who I care about, so they won't have to worry about repercussions or being embarrassed. And frankly, so I won't get sued. Because isn't it just like a bully to try to get back at someone they have already beaten up?

That not going to happen to me. Not ever again.

Bullying in the workplace is either at an all-time high; or we are just more aware of the bullying; or both. I believe in the latter. I am convinced that not much is being done to stop the bullies. I believe this because it is what I witnessed, what I've read and from my research.

According to the *"2017 U.S. Workplace Bullying Survey,"* almost 60 percent of U.S. workers are affected by workplace bullying. Look at these statistics from the survey that is now almost three years old,

- 19 percent of Americans are bullied, another 19 per-

cent witness it
- 61 percent of Americans are aware of abusive conduct in the workplace
- 60.4 million Americans are affected by it
- 70 percent of perpetrators are men; 60 percent of targets are women
- Hispanics are the most frequently bullied ethnic group
- 61 percent of bullies are bosses, the majority (63 percent) operate alone
- 40 percent of bullied targets are believed to suffer adverse health effects
- 29 percent of targets remain silent about their experiences
- 71 percent of employer reactions are harmful to targets
- 60 percent of coworker reactions are harmful to targets
- To stop it, 65 percent of targets lose their original jobs
- 77 percent of Americans support enacting a new law
- 46 percent report worsening of work relationships, post-Trump election

Because the United States is doing nothing to stop workplace bullying, I'm convinced these statistics are getting worse. Look at the last bullet point. If we elect "Leaders" who openly bully, what else can we expect.

I was dismayed when I read the *"2017 Bullying Survey"* because I was targeted by three workplace bullies at my last job. I decided to leave that job in June 2017. I was bullied into retirement.

I was depressed when I left a job I loved, and I became more depressed when I read the survey. Because I was so stunned that so many workers are living through what I had just gone through.

Why wasn't something being done about these bullies?

I consider myself a fighter, a trailblazer who broke barriers in radio, television and political reporting. Yet I didn't really fight the bullies. I didn't file a complaint; I just quit. I wasn't brave; I was a coward. I didn't do what was right. I let them get away with it. I'm sorry. I wish I had been stronger, but I was so beaten up and beaten down I just had to flee.

I am writing this book with hope that it will help you. While it is painful to remember and write about it; its important. Because we need to fight them and stop them.

When you read these stories, you will know we all struggle with workplace bullies. And you will know you have options and you can survive.

As I was suffering and trying to survive my bullies; I knew friends, family and colleagues who were dealing with their own real life, living and breathing Bully-Demons.

This book is about the targets and their stories.

At first glance it seems as if Pearl, Laura, Anthony, Gloria, and Carol have nothing in common.

Laura is a 30-something English major, Anthony is in his late teens and just beginning his first job, and entering college, Pearl is a 50-year-old experienced, federal office worker, I was a television journalist turned marketing manager and video producer and Carol is a military veteran, and an award-winning community relations, marketing professional.

We are a diverse group with one thing in common, we were all targeted by workplace bullies. And we all lost something of ourselves in the process of surviving. We lost jobs, we lost confidence, a sense of self-worth. And so much more that I can't even put into words.

As painful as it is to remember my bullying, it's worth it if it helps you realize that you are not alone.

I hope it helps.

PART TWO

OUR STORIES

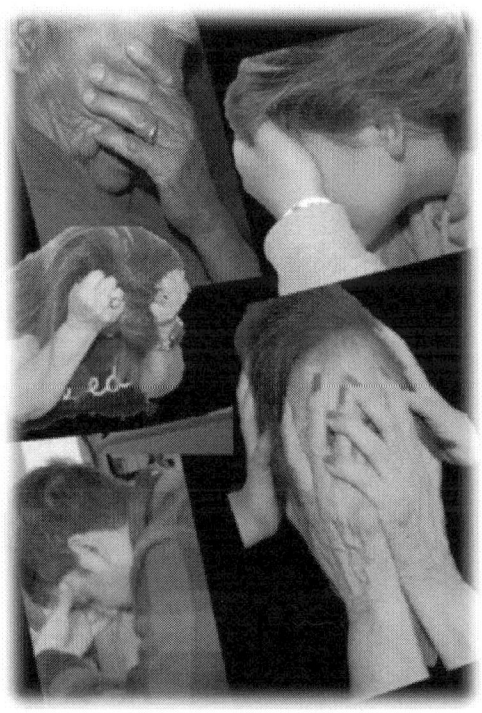

CHAPTER FIVE

LAURA'S STORY

" 71 percent of employer reactions are harmful to targets."

2017 U.S. Workplace Bullying Survey

The Jealous Green-Eyed Monster Bully

"When you're a secretary in a brewery, it's pretty hard to make-believe you're anything else. Everything is BEER."

Eve Harrington, *"All About Eve"*

Tall, beautiful and smart is the only way I can describe Laura. When she walks in a room heads turn to look at her. An English major, she worked her way up through several positions before joining our office. She is an excellent writer and copy editor and extremely well-liked and she excelled at every project. She eventually worked her way up into a key public relations position.

Change is inevitable. My career and Laura's changed when a new manager was appointed to oversee our office.

He was, to put it simply, incompetent. He was and probably still is an incompetent, passive aggressive bully. And this is ironic, he was not the worst change that happened. He hired someone who made Laura's work life and mine unbearable.

Suddenly we had two bullies in upper management, who spent their days micromanaging our office and basically destroying all the positive work we had accomplished before they arrived.

They destroyed and they bullied.

They destroyed great work relationships with other departments, they killed goodwill, they reassigned key projects, that were then ignored or mismanaged.

They were asserting their power, making the office "Theirs" not "Ours". And they achieved this by bullying the staff, Remember, this is a public sector office. Supported by tax dollars. In the private sector, where I worked for 20 years, if you made money and were successful you didn't have to worry too much about personal jealousy and petty ego.

Higher education breeds a whole different level of nincompoops. He was Dumb. She was Dumber. These two were idiots! And they were mean. And they bullied.

The bullying of Laura began when the male manager hired a female department head. It was clear from the start that she was jealous of the younger, more popular, more competent Laura.

Here are some of the ways they began bullying Laura and making her work life miserable.

They made her responsible for writing dozens of reports that they didn't read. They required that she produce dozens of "talking points" documents that they did not use. They changed her staffing assignments without telling her, and then they fired one of her productive staff members when she was on vacation.

Every day for four years she was abused, yelled at and demoralized. Finally, she had enough. She documented her treatment and filed a complaint with Human Resources. HR did nothing. The head of Human Resources reported Laura's complaint to the two bullies and their boss the University President.

Laura's treatment worsened.

Most of the staff were aware of Laura's treatment. One by one staff members walked upstairs to complain to the president.

While they all stood up to complain about the two managers, I curled up in the fetal position under my desk. Okay, I didn't do that but that's what it felt like. (That story in another chapter)

The president promised the staff that he would take some action. He did not. He didn't want to. He was a big bully himself. He set the tone for the entire department and the entire university. The managers followed his lead. And the culture of bullying was justified and repeated in offices on the entire campus. It was sick.

The Department scheduled a staff retreat. After a day of listening to endless experts, the demoralized staff was invited to a wine and cheese, after-retreat gathering.

That was when Laura's male manager drunkenly walked up to her, moved his face close to hers, spitting as he spoke and said, "See, I'm still here and they aren't going to do anything to me, and you're fucked."

He then spilled wine on her dress.

There were witnesses. Nothing was done to the manager. Not long after that incident Laura left her job. She is now an extremely successful public relations manager.

The office continued to be horribly mismanaged following Laura's departure. It didn't seem to matter. The two bullies remained. They had no management experience, no people skills, no talent, and no personalities. When I left my job because of my endless bullying by those two they were both still there mismanaging the department and wasting hundreds of thousands of tax dollars a year on their inadequate marketing and public relation's failures.

Lessons Learned from Laura

Laura did all the right things. She documented her treatment. She complained to Human Resources. She reported her treatment to the Bully's supervisor. She completed every task assigned. But most important she kept her job, updated her resume and looked for a better job. It is so important to keep your job while searching for a better position. You don't want the bullies to force you to quit. Searching for a job while you are unemployed puts you in a position of weakness. You want to remain strong. You want to win; the bullies are the losers.

What the Experts Recommend

"Do hold the employer accountable for putting you in harm's way. It is not your personal responsibility as the victim to fix the mess you did not start. Employers control the work environment. When you are injured as a result of exposure to that environment, make the employer own the responsibility to fix it."

From the "*Workplace Bully Institute 3-Step Target Action Plan*"

That sounds great but it doesn't always work that way. Not yet. Laura's real-life case proves it. Some employers don't want anything to change, and they won't unless legally forced to.

I found this tip in an article in the *"MUSE"*, written by Stav Ziv, *"Don't let Workplace Bullies Win..."*

"Keep a journal of the who, what, when, where, why of things that happen," says **Catherine Mattice** Zundel, CEO of Civility Partners, "If you're in a staff meeting and the bullying occurs, then go back to your desk and write down who else was in the staff meeting, what was said, why was it said, and try to just put in as much detail as you can around kind of the facts of the situation."

Notes about the Quote

I began this chapter with a quote from the movie, *"All About Eve,"* starring actress Bette Davis. The Academy Award-Winning movie was adapted from a short story "The Wisdom of Eve," written by Mary Orr. The screenplay was written by Joseph L. Mankiewicz, and it has some of the best lines in film history; and a plot that relates to bullies and my story about Laura and the Green-Eyed Jealous Monster Bully. If you are unfamiliar with the 1950 movie, please check it out.

The film is about a younger actress, Eve, who befriends a successful Broadway star, Margot Channing. Margot has everything that Eve covets. Eve lies, cheats, and quietly bullies her way into Margot's life and career. Eve gets what she wants, Margot's part in a successful stage production, but she is miserable in the end.

Laura's boss bullies were so jealous of her, she was and is everything they are not and never will be. But Laura is happy to be far away from those bullies.

◆ ◆ ◆

CHAPTER SIX

GLORIA'S STORY

"29 percent of targets remain silent about their experiences."

"2017 U.S. Workplace Bullying Survey"

The University Workplace Bullies

"If you are going through Hell, keep going"

Winston Churchill

I was a political reporter for 20 years when I went back to school to earn my master's degree while working full time as a political correspondent in Washington D.C., but I felt the decision was going to help me achieve a more stable future.

I knew I wouldn't be on television when I was an older woman. My long-term goal was to work at a university, and I knew I needed a master's degree if I was going to be taken seriously.

I moved from Washington to Sacramento, CA. where I worked for five years as a political reporter; and for an additional five as managing editor at the ABC-News affiliate.

I managed a staff of reporters and I was responsible for on-air and online news content. I applied for and was hired by a Sacramento University to work as their news director in public affairs.

I was thrilled to accept the job.

I didn't know I would endure 11 years of bullying by three key upper level managers.

When I took the job, I had hoped to produce and write positive academic stories about students and faculty. I wanted to work there forever.

Wow. Was I wrong!

My first bully at the university was a woman who enjoyed putting her managers, on the spot. She was a yeller and a bully, and everybody knew it.

Once in a director's meeting she was questioning a colleague; and the woman became flustered and began to fidget and her face became red. That was it. The bully snapped, "Why are you nervous, why is your face red?" The woman, Annie, stammered and said, "I don't know." And the bully yelled, "No, you don't know. This is just stupid. You are stupid!"

I opened my mouth to speak up and she pointed her finger at me and said, "You don't want to go there!"

And for one of the first times in my career I shut my mouth. I was ashamed for not speaking up for my colleague. It became a pattern with me; one that included self-loathing.

Many times, I would be in my office working on projects and my phone would ring and the bully would call, and she would just begin screaming at me. I had no idea why. Once I said, what did I do wrong. And she screamed, "That's it! You don't know anything!"

When the university president decided to reorganize and move our department to another area I was thrilled. Maybe now I could relax and work for a normal manager. It was the worst change I ever endured in my career.

I didn't know that the new vice president didn't want me on his team. He wanted to hire some of his cronies from the local newspaper who were all losing their jobs.

Even though I had worked for years to earn my position, he began quietly harassing me, and bullying me so I would resign.

It became a war; with him bombarding me with numerous assignments and mental abuse and me refusing to surrender; I just went along accepting all his attacks just to prove he wasn't going to get rid of me.

My office was downstairs, his office was upstairs. My phone would ring, and he would snap, "Get up here."

I use crutches to walk. I would walk to the opposite end of the building to take the elevator upstairs rather than taking the stairs which were near my office door and his. I didn't want to trip and fall on the stairs.

More than once he said to me, in private. "You to get up here faster." My mouth dropped open. I thought, did he just say that.

More than once he said. "You took too long; I don't need you anymore."

Many, many times he would ask me one or two questions, nothing that couldn't have been dealt with on the phone and then he would dismiss me.

He decided not to hire an office assistant. So, for a year, despite a heavy workload, I would have to walk to the front of the office to respond to people just walking in the door.

After a year I was demoted.

He hired the wife of a friend from the newspaper. She had no management experience, no public affairs experience and no advanced degree. And this is illegal, she did not have to apply for the job or go through the hiring committee process. She was appointed. And when she was promoted it was done quietly without posting the job or accepting other applications.

I had survived three years of bullying by the female bully. One year with the male bully. Now I had two bullies who would devote much of their time inventing projects for me that seemed to be impossible to complete.

After my demotion, many of my top-level projects were given to other staff members. These were projects that I had excelled at. I had helped save the university from a lawsuit; I had expertly managed an officer-involved shooting. My list of accomplishment is documented.

Eventually, I lost all my projects and given very little to do. This was their way of setting the groundwork to lay me off.

I was in a panic.

I was approaching age 55, my 75-year-old father, my 20-year-old daughter and her newborn baby were all living with me and depending on me.

How could I be in this predicament?

I needed to work at least one more year to be eligible for retirement benefits, including health care.

I did the only thing I could do; I e-mailed the university president, asking to be reassigned to another department.

He e-mailed back. He would see what he could do.

He could do anything. I wasn't transferred; but was given a long-term project. This gave me another couple of years so I could make it to an early (unwanted) retirement.

So, I stayed. I took care of my family. And I endured.

I had my marketing project; and won three awards for the university television show I created and produced.

But the bullies never stopped harassing me. I had no support. I was required to shoot video and edit all my stories.

Let me be clear, we had people sitting around the office with nothing to do and I was shooting and editing and writing and producing seven half hour television and online shows.

They wanted me to fail. Instead, I won awards.

I was moved to a small dark workspace; it was depressing and horrible. My desk was not a real desk, I had to sit with the corner of a table digging into my stomach.

I requested a motorized cart so I wouldn't have to carry my gear long distances. That request was denied. Other staff members have their own carts. Why was I denied a cart? I use crutches, I am legally disabled, and I was denied a cart. I had to carry about 15 pounds of gear.

My computer wouldn't handle all the large video files. My software would crash a couple of times a day. I requested a better computer. It was denied.

I was told that the bully said I was NEVER to get a better computer. "Let her win awards," he said. "with her old computer."

They hired a white male to take my former job, director of multimedia job, that was the position I was assigned to after my first demotion.

I had been demoted again, this time to an executive producer position.

The new hire was kind and professional. He ordered a video editing computer and secretly gave it to me.

Still, I was in hell.

And *"People in Hell want Ice Water."*

Winston Churchill said, "If you are going through Hell, keep going."

I decided to take Sir Winston's advice.

After 11 years at the University, they took one more shot at me. I was going to be audited. And then I was going to be demoted again, with a major pay cut.

I looked at the numbers, I could retire and make more money with my retirement and pensions than if I stayed and continued to work alone, shooting all my own videos with no promotion or support. I left. I was replaced by people with less experience and no advanced degrees.

According to the *"2017 Workplace Bullying Survey"* the way I reacted to my bullying and the decisions I made are like others. I decided to include the chart and the text that explains how we lose our jobs because of bullying.

2017 Workplace Bullying Survey

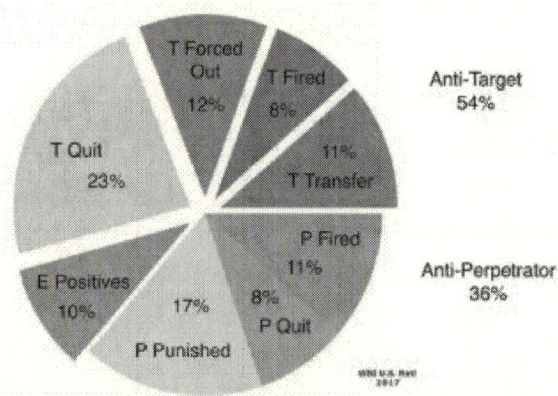

"... once a person is targeted for bullying – a choice made by the perpetrator(s) – that person has a 5 out of 10 chance of losing her or his livelihood. If one adds the 11 percent of targets who had to transfer to retain employment, 65 percent of targets had to leave the job they loved for no cause.

Furthermore, the target is driven to quit. Voluntary quitting (23 percent) is usually based on escalating health problems that families and physicians recognize, then encourage the target to leave the job.

But 12 percent of quitting is based on decisions made after work conditions become untenable, so cruel as to drive a rational person to escape. Constructive discharge is the goal for many perpetrators.

Terminations (8 percent) of the skilled but threatening (to bullies) targets are typically based on fabricated lies."

❖ ❖ ❖

What I Did Right

Nothing!

Just kidding. My sense of humor has helped me through my life. I did one thing right. I kept great notes. One of my television bosses once said to me, always take good notes. "The person who takes the best notes, wins! In Court!"

I am using my notes to write this book and I hope they help you feel better just by knowing you are not alone.

What I Did Wrong

I did not file a complaint with Human Resources. I did not file an official complaint with my boss's supervisors. I suffered in silence.

I did not show my documentation to my supervisors and confront them. When others in the office were complaining about the bullying, I did not join them.

My worst mistake, I quit. I left a job I loved.

What the Experts Recommend

The Workplace Bully institute recommends that we *"Take Time Off to Heal & Launch a Counterattack"*. I wish I had done this. I did not take care of myself, mentally or physically. I pushed myself harder and harder, with the hope that I could convince them to give up.

Here is a quote from their website. "Research state and federal legal options (in a quarter of bullying cases, discrimination plays a role). Talk to an attorney. Maybe a demand letter can be written. Look for internal policies (harassment, violence, respect) for violations to report (fully expecting retaliation). Start job search for next position."

About the Quotes

I am a political nerd and a history fanatic. I enjoy reading about Winston Churchill; and of all the advice I'm sharing I like Sir Winston's advice best. "If you are going through Hell, keep going."

I'm adding my advice, RUN! Run as fast as you are financially able to run away from the bullies.

CHAPTER SEVEN

ANTHONY'S STORY

"60 percent of coworker reactions are harmful to targets."

"2017 U.S. Workplace Bullying Survey"

The Passive-Aggressive Bully

"So that was Mrs. Lundegaard on the floor in there. And I guess that was your accomplice in the woodchipper. And those three people in Brainerd. And for what? For a little bit of money. There's more to life than a little money, you know. Don't you know that? And here ya are, and it's a beautiful day. Well, I just don't understand it.

Marge Gunderson *"Fargo"*

Anthony was 17 years old when he was hired by the local school district to work in the recreational sports office. It's the place where students, their families and community members go to register for after-school sports. It is a busy, thriving office; a fun place to work. The job was going to help Anthony pay for his college education, for his textbooks, clothing and food. He was living at home; but needed the money.

The bullying by his supervisor began almost immediately after he was hired.

The Bully, in this case was a 50-year-old female supervisor, who was firmly entrenched in the school district. We will call her Dolores; she was well-thought-of and had a good reputation among clients and school officials. But her reputation among her young staff was entirely different.

I sat down with Anthony on a sunny, November day and he told me his story.

The following first-person narrative is Anthony's.

One of our biggest events was hosting an annual softball tournament, people would come in and reserve the space and get placed on the roster. We would take their checks; then Dolores, and only Dolores would take the checks and place the teams on the schedule.

One team manager came in late on Friday right when we were closing and handed me a check, I put it in a drawer, then closed and went home.

I got a long text, all in CAPS the next day. It was Dolores screaming at me because the team manager was in the office and they couldn't find his check.

I sent her a text message and apologized, telling her the check was in the drawer.

The nasty long texts continued all weekend, they were berating, mean and insulting.

On Monday, she walked into the office, walked right by me, didn't look at me or talk to me. She ignored me all week. She didn't talk about what I did wrong; or tell me she received my texts or my apologies.

She didn't speak to me all week. It was stressful to be at work or be around her. It felt like walking on eggshells. It was a very toxic environment. I walked back to her office one afternoon to ask her for some forms I needed to help a customer register for one of our programs, and she snapped at me, "I'll take care of this!"

Her nastiness got worst from then on. I was on her bad list. Everything I did was wrong. I was responsible for managing our website, basic customer service skills and creating a database of all our customers. We would send a mass e-mail to advertise all the sports we offer. She criticized all my work. I couldn't do anything right in her eyes. She would roll her eyes and say things like, "That is not the right way to do it." But she never sat down with me like a normal supervisor and trained me. There was no guidance.

I was a young student, with little work experience. Her insults made me feel stupid. She would belittle me. I began to think I was stupid and doubted my abilities and I felt that I would never be able to find a better job.

So, I stayed. And I was bullied. And I hated it.

Dolores had a rule that if somebody came into the office asking for her, she didn't want me to tell them that she was available. she wanted me to walk back to her desk, tell her who it was and if she didn't want to talk to them, she would have me tell them she was "not here because she's in a meeting."

After an entire week of dealing with her hostility and her passive-aggressive attitude towards me I had it.

Someone came in and asked for her; and instead of letting her know who it was I told them they can go back and see her.

Dolores didn't like that. She came up to me in a rage and told me that was disrespectful; that the person I sent back could have been a killer, and she might have been harmed.

The person I sent back had talked to her face-to-face last week. But she loved blowing things out of portion and making me look like the inconsiderate one. That was the final straw for me. I had so much built-up frustration towards her. I told her she has made this week miserable for me.

I asked her why she wouldn't talk to me or look at me? I explained that we were not communicating with each other effectively. And I told her it was wrong to treat people like this; and that she needs to get better at talking to her employees instead of trying to make them so miserable they just want to quit.

She saidthat she was upset with me about not putting the check in the right place and it made her, and our department look bad and couldn't believe that I didn't even apologize for the situation.

I did apologize, profusely.

After that discussion, we apologize to each other and the next day at work she was back to normal and everything was fine. But then I started noticing that she would do things that affected my job in a very subtle way.

She began cutting my hours. That was the worst part of her bullying. I was losing money to get through school, to pay my car insurance and for books. And to top it off she was giving my work hours to her relatives.

She hired her son and gave him the website responsibilities; she hired her son's girlfriend and she was responsible for compiling the database for all our employees. I just sat there, working less and less.

When I asked if I could work more hours, she said, "Why, you must have lots of money saved from the three years you've been working here!"

And then there were the racist remarks. Here are two examples. It's difficult to describe just how bad the racist atmosphere was that was created by Delores.

She is white, I'm half white and half Mexican.

One day Dolores and her assistant were talking about tattoos. Dolores said to me, "Anthony where is your tattoo?"

"I don't have one," I said. "My dad and grandpa hate them so I'm not getting one."

And she replied, "I thought all Mexicans got tattoos."

Another time, one of the student workers put some cash from a parent that on top of a file cabinet by mistake. Everyone was searching for the money, but we couldn't find it.

Finally, the student was called in and she showed us where it was.

When we were walking to our cars that night Delores said to me, "I was sure she stole it, I was ready to call the cops, because she is black and that's what blacks do, they steal."

We live in a very diverse community; we have a melting pot of nationalities and ethnicities. People would come in sometimes and they were clearly struggling with their English language skills. Delores always refused to pronounce their names properly. Once she said, "I can't pronounce that," after a Southeast Asian man repeated his name to her.

"I'll just call you this, instead." And she said something just awful to the man that embarrassed all of us.

Anthony stayed with the school district and his job, but he watched many other students quit because of Delores. School officials never did anything to stop her bullying behavior. What ended her reign of terror was a stroke that forced her to retire.

❖ ❖ ❖

What Anthony Did Right

After a week of bullying, Anthony confronted Delores. That confrontation forced the bully to stop her passive-aggressive behavior in the short-term. But in the long-term Anthony lost money when his hours were cut.

What Anthony Could Have Done

Anthony could have documented all the bullying incidents; and filed a complaint with Delores's supervisor. While there are no Anti-Workplace Bully Protection laws; there are laws against nepotism. Delores could have been in trouble for hiring her relatives.

What the Experts Recommend

"Check your mental health with a professional (not the employer's EAP). Get emotionally stable enough to make a clear-headed decision to stay and fight, or to leave for your health's sake. Your humanity makes you vulnerable; it is not a weakness, but a sign of superiority. Work Trauma, by definition, is an overwhelming, extraordinary experience."

"Workplace Bully Institute's 3-Step Target Action Plan"

About the Quote

I use this quote for Anthony's story because, I wonder why bullies bully. Do they torture targets "for a little bit of money?" It hurts us so much what do **they** get out of it. Is it for the power? Is it Money? Just like those "bad guys" in *"Fargo"* is it for a little bit of money? Are they evil? Delores had the power, why hurt Anthony?

And I'm quoting Marge now, "And it's a beautiful day. Well I just don't understand it."

CHAPTER EIGHT

PEARL'S STORY

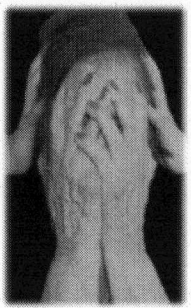

"61 percent of bullies are bosses, the majority (63 percent) operate alone."

"2017 U.S. Workplace Bullying Survey"

The New Supervisor Bully

"I am mad. I'm always losing things and hiding things and I can never find them; I don't know where I've put them."

Paula Alquist Anton, *"Gaslight"*

Pearl was a mid-level federal government office worker; she was well-respected and popular among staff and managers alike.

She was organized, efficient and smart; her career wasn't her top priority, she put her husband and children and grandchildren first. She worked hard, went home on time and always did her job; she tried to stay out of office politics.

She became a bully's target when a new manager joined her department. Her Bully, Janet had transferred to California from Arizona. The bullying of most of the staff began shortly after Janet made her first speech to the staff. Janet promised that there would be very few changes for the staff or the way the office was organized.

The bully broke that promise the very next day. She began changing everything about the office immediately. And she did it without consulting with the people who had efficiently been running the office for years.

One of Pearl's job duties was to work with staff and outside vendors when open enrollment for health care coverage took place once a year.

It was a huge week-long event, with health insurance companies setting up tables packed with brochures and information to entice workers to sign up with their companies.

Pearl managed the schedule, booked the insurance vendors, reserve the space and worked to publicize the event.

The day before the big event, Janet told Pearl, "You are going to have to move the open enrollment event. We are going to use the room for something else."

Pearl was stunned, and speechless. Then she panicked! Pearl didn't argue with her supervisor; she didn't make a scene. She got on the phone and booked another room. She wrote a note that said, "OPEN ENROLLMENT MOVED!" She made copies and posted them in many places as possible. She arranged for a student intern to help direct staff and the vendors to the new location, it was exhausting and stressful to move the event that had been planned for a year.

The next day, Janet said, "Well Pearl, you really pulled that off." Then she said, "The birthday party we had in the conference room was nice."

Pearl was livid. All that work for a birthday party that could have been held anywhere.

One day Janet walked into the office and said, "I don't like the location of these brochures."

Pearl said, "When employees come in asking us about benefits all we have to do is point at the brochures, they answer all the questions people have and more."

Janet said, "I don't care, move them. Put them outside, they just look like clutter in the office."

Pearl spent the next day rearranging the brochures outside the office door. When Janet arrived for work, she looked at Pearl and said, "Why are the brochures in the hallway?"

Pearl was dumbfounded.

"You told me to move them, so I moved them." Pearl said evenly.

"I most certainly did not tell you that," The bully said. Please put them back in the office."

Janet turned and left.

A few hours later another staff member asked Pearl, "Aren't you going to move the brochures back into the office?"

"No, I will not," Pearl said. "She told me to move them, I moved them. I won't move them back."

Because Pearl was respected and so well liked a couple of other workers moved all the brochures back into the office lobby.

The *Gaslighting* of Pearl continued for the next two years. She was not alone the bully tormented the entire staff. The woman who promised that there would be no real changes worked non-stop to get the entire staff to transfer or quit.

Pearl, who was respected and love and who knew how to run the office with her eyes closed decided to retire. She didn't want to deal with bullies ever again.

◆ ◆ ◆

What Pearl Did Right

Pearl never lost her temper; she was always even tempered and professional. She continued to be Pearl, cool, calm and efficient; even though she was suffering from the bullying.

What She Could Have Done

Pearl could have asked for a transferred to another department. She could have confronted her bully. She was so well-liked, there is a good chance the Bully could have backed off.

What the Experts Say

"Expose the Bully." This is the advice from the Workplace Bully Institute." They say, "The real risk was sustained when you were first targeted (Targets lose their job - involuntarily or by choice for their health's sake - in 77.7% of cases). It is no riskier to attempt to dislodge the bully. Retaliation is a certainty. Have your escape route planned."

"Workplace Bully Institute's 3-

Step Target Action Plan"

I'm not crazy about this advice. But as a former target and survivor. I agree, if you are strong and can take more abuse as you look for another job.

About the Quote

Gaslight is a 1944 film, kind of a creepy, psychological thriller. The movie was adapted from Patrick Hamilton's 1938 play *Gas Light*. It's about a woman whose husband slowly manipulates her into believing that she is going insane. The movie starred Ingrid Bergman and Charles Boyer. He was broke and needed her money; and he was having an affair with a younger woman. I never could understand why any man would not want Ingrid Bergman. Just like I can't understand why anyone would bully Pearl.

Every now and then someone will use the phrase, "I'm being gaslighted." Pearl's bully was Gaslighting her for sure. When a manager gives you an order, then realizes it was a dumb decision, the easiest way for then to get out of it is to deny they ever said it.

I was gaslighted several times, as well. When my bully managers lied and denied they had given me an order, I would pull out my notepad, which I always carried and quote the conversation and the day the order was given. Did that help me? NO! They hated that. And the bullying increased. Did that make me crazy like the wife in *Gaslight*? Absolutely.

CHAPTER NINE

CAROL'S STORY

"61 percent of Americans are aware of abusive conduct in the workplace."

"2017 U.S. Workplace Bullying Survey"

Bullying the Whistle Blower

"You know, Burke, I don't know which species is worse. You don't see them fucking each other over for a goddamn percentage."

Ellen Ripley, *"Aliens"*

I met Carol when we both worked in Washington, D.C. She was fresh out of the Navy and getting ready to marry the man of her dreams, a handsome lieutenant named Bill. She was hired to work as a fill-in reporter in the news bureau where I worked. We quickly became friends. She was nice, happy, a very positive, spiritual person and a pleasure to be around.

She also has a very impressive resume. She was a radio and television star when she was in the United States Navy. She was on the American Forces Network (AFN). The AFN worldwide radio and television broadcast network serves American servicemembers, Department of Defense and other U.S. government civilians and their families stationed at bases overseas, as well as U.S. Navy ships at sea. AFN broadcasts popular American radio and television programs from the major U.S. networks. Her reports were broadcast all over the world. From Washington, the newly married couple moved to the Southwest and Carol became a local legend. She oversaw the Veteran's Day Parades in her area. She became an award-winning marketing and public affairs guru.

We kept in touch throughout the years and visited each other and we remain friends.

Carol, a veteran, of course befriended and supported other veterans and the great, caring doctors and others who began complaining, loudly about the quality of treatment veterans were receiving or not receiving at U.S. hospitals.

That's when her troubles began. Carol was perceived as a Whistleblower by her supervisors. She was friends with them so she must be one. The Veteran's Administration Whistleblowers were sending facts and figures to lawmakers and the newspapers documenting how long it was taking for veterans to receive medical care. The delays were almost criminal. Bottom line, veterans weren't getting health care.

By law, Whistleblowers are supposed to be protected from retaliation. We all now know that is not what happen. Carole was bullied, and tormented. She was demoted and removed from her position. She was given a desk in the basement.

During this time, she called me to ask what I had done when I was being bullied. I told her, I'm not as brave as you, or as young. I'm just hanging in here. I advised her to go over the heads of the bullies as I had done. But that didn't work for her. Carol's bullying increased.

She called me again in a couple of weeks, we chatted then she told me this story. At this point they had moved her into the basement, and they had limited her time with other employees. Any work that was assigned was rejected as below standards and incomplete.

She said, she was so stressed out that she would arrive home from work, go straight to her bedroom, lie down on the bed and fall asleep. She was ignoring her husband and two children. She was so distressed and distraught she felt like she couldn't cope with anything.

The next morning her alarm would go off and she would jump up and go back to work in the same clothes she wore the day before. I was stunned. My happy, perfect, strong, perky friend was an award-winning Navy veteran and she was being treated horribly by bullies!

Those same bullies eventually pushed Carol out of a job she loved so much. And it's taken her years to recover. But she has recovered. She has written a book and it may become a film! Carol you are my hero.

PART THREE

HOW TO STOP
WORK BULLIES

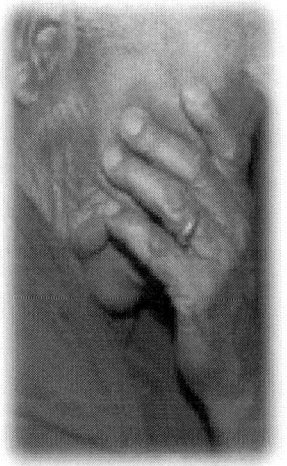

"77 percent of Americans support enacting a new law."

2017 U.S. Workplace Bullying Survey

CHAPTER TEN

LET'S STOP THEM

The stories I've shared are just a few examples of workplace bullying. Think about Laura's, Anthony's, Pearl's, Carol's and Gloria's stories multiplied again and again and again. To the tune of millions of American workers.

We have a problem, Houston. And it's not in space. it's here, on earth, at work.

Workplace bullying is hurting the best of us; while the bullies thrive like a Cancer. Am I being over-dramatic? Of course. But I'm angry. Aren't you?

Here's the worst part. After years of research and surveys and the complying of facts, the United States has not made progress toward passage of anti-bullying workplace legislation.

WHAT? WHY?

The **WBI**, **Workplace Bullying Institute** has work diligently to make progress towards passage of the anti-bullying *"Healthy Workplace Bill"*. **WBI** researchers have been studying workplace bullying and conducting surveys since 1997.

The problem is serious and growing.

Still, strong workplace anti-bullying legislation has not been passed by any state legislature. And it has only been "introduced" in 30 states. An all-encompassing federal law does not exist.

Let's say that again, "An all-encompassing federal law does not exist."

Here is the where we stand in the United States of America. This information is from the Healthy Workplace Bill website,

"The U.S. is the last of the western democracies NOT to have a law forbidding bullying-like conduct in the workplace. Scandinavian nations have explicit anti-bullying laws. Many of the EU nations have substantially more legal employee protections, which compel employers to prevent or correct bullying."

Britain is the place where the phrase "workplace bullying," was born. This happened in the 1980's and 1990's. Since then Great Britain has enacted stronger and broader anti-harassment laws than the U.S. to cover bullying. In 2005, Ireland passed a strong health and safety code to address bullying.

CHAPTER ELEVEN

THE HEALTHY WORKPLACE BILL

At the beginning of this book I wrote, "There is a **"Workplace Bullying Institute"** and a *"Healthy Workplace Bill"* and a *"National Campaign"* to make workplace bullying illegal.

Like Obi Wan Kenobi in Star Wars IV, *"... they are out only hope."*

Out hope lies with the people who established the **Workplace Bullying Institute**; they are responsible for conducting their research and producing the *"Workplace Bullying Surveys."*

Here is some background, since 2003, the *"Healthy Workplace Bill"* has been introduced in several state legislatures. The legislation would create protections again workplace bullying. Here is an excerpt from the bill,"

"The critical definition in this cause of action is "abusive work environment," which: "exists when the defendant, acting with *malice*, subjects an employee to *abusive conduct* so severe that it causes *tangible harm* to the employee."

One of the authors of the bill says he was extremely careful when drafting the legal definitions of bullying. Here more,

"Malice is defined as the desire to cause pain, injury, or distress to another."

The supporters of the bill say, "this is a high legal standard, and it is likely that some targets of harmful, intentional bullying will encounter difficulty in meeting it."

So, this will limit lawsuits. Right? Apparently not! According to critics.

Critics of the anti-bulling workplace legislation, including state chapters of the Chamber of Commerce and management-side employment lawyers lobby again the measure saying passage will cause a flood of frivolous lawsuits from us, the bullied!

Even though the measure has been carefully written; it has not been passed into law.

Even my home state of California, that my East Coast Friends call the "Left Wing Liberal Coast" only passed a "watered-down" version of the bill.

On **Sept. 9, 2014,** Gov. Jerry Brown signed **AB 2053** into law, This bill was NOT the Healthy Workplace Bill that would have encouraged employers to act to stop bullying or face liability. Ab 2053 required training. That's all!

As a manager, working at a State supported University I was required to take that training. It was online course that I took in my office while eating lunch. My Bully-Bosses were also required to take that training.

They continued to bully me.

CHAPTER TWELVE

THIS IS WORTH REPEATING
There is NO Federal Anti-Bullying Law

Currently, if you are severely bullied you can file a claim that you have suffered mental or physical harm; but you must prove it in court.

Here is a quote from the "Better Workplaces – Better World" website. "Bullying is actionable under federal law only when the basis for it is tied to a protected category, such as race or sex, explained Jessica Westerman, an attorney with Katz, Marshall & Banks in Washington, D.C. Specifically, Title VII of the Civil Rights Act of 1964 prohibits harassment on the basis of color, national origin, race, religion and sex. Other federal laws prohibit such behavior on the basis of age, disability and genetic information."

I could have sued my bullies because I am old or because I am legally disabled; but what about the rest of us? Why are there no protections? In addition, I would have had to prove the bullying; they would have denied it, called me a liar, forced co-worker to lie and turn against me.

I spoke with Carol about her fight against her bullies and she said, "Fighting takes everything out of you, you never recover. It's a high price to pay and not really worth it."

So, the bullies win.

CHAPTER THIRTEEN

LET'S BEAT THE BULLIES

You want some good news?

"Sioux City Iowa is the first school district in the nation to address workplace bullying for their adult employees," according to the *"Healthy Workplace Bill"* website.

Let's all move to Sioux City, Iowa!

That's it for the good news people.

Join the Grass Roots Campaign Now

If you want to know what we can do, here it is, we can work together to speaking loudly and in unison for passage of the *"Healthy Workplace Bill."*

Right now, the authors and supporters of the legislation are working on campaigns in individual states. But there is no movement to get a federal bill passed.

When I write a sad story, or produce a podcast or video about a tragic "social issue" people always say, "What I can do about it?"

Well I have an answer, go to *"The Healthy Workplace Bill's"* website: https://healthyworkplacebill.org/

And **Join the Campaign Now.**

Nothing is going to happen if we just quietly suffer in silence. We got to organize (**The Workplace Bullying Institute** has done that work); and get vocal and get loud.

"Targets Unite!" See you all at the Rally. What Rally? The Rally's we are going to organize in 2020!

About The Author

G**loria Moraga** is a former television journalist, and digital content creator and communicator. As the chief executive director of **Moraga Media, s**he produces videos and creates all forms of digital content, including a Podcast, *"One-On-One – Communications in the Digital Age."* Two YouTube Channels, *"The Gloria Moraga Channel";* and the *"Pinch of Mexican Channel"*, and two websites, gloriamoraga.com and pinchofmexican.com. She is currently writing a cookbook featuring her family's special Mexican Food recipes.

ACKNOWLEDGMENTS

I want to thank Alan Miller for editing this book. Alan is a real newsman, a great professor and a wonderful editor. I want to thank Laura, Carole, Pearl and Anthony, the workers also known as targets who took the time to tell me their stories for this book and my podcast.

I also thank those who are responsible for establishing the **Workplace Bullying Institute.**

My goal was to write a series of blogs and produce podcasts on Workplace Bullying. I decided to tackle this book after reading the works of **Gary Namie, PhD** and his wife **Ruth Namie, PhD.**

Dr. Ruth Namie has a doctorate in clinical psychology. Her personal experience became the impetus for the U.S. workplace bullying movement. She is now the definitive expert on the devastating effects of bullying on targeted workers.

Dr. Gary Namie is a social psychologist and widely regarded as North America's foremost authority on Workplace Bullying. In 2007, 2010, 2014 and 2017 Dr. Namie wrote, and Zogby Analytics conducted, the most frequently cited, largest-ever, scientific U.S. survey of Workplace Bullying. Along with his wife, Ruth, they wrote the popular books, *The Bully-Free Workplace* (Wiley, 2011) and *The Bully At Work* 2nd ed. (Sourcebooks, 2009).

Thank you for your inspiring work.

Also thank you to my models, who appear throughout the

CALL TO ACTION

Please take a moment to review this book. I appreciate all feedback.

I have created a special "Targeted by Work Bullies" page on my website, gloriamoraga.com. I am updating content and information about the "Healthy Workplace Bill," and more.

I am also producing a series of videos and podcast episodes on this topic. Please watch, download, listen and share. You can find all the links on my website.

The book was produced by Moraga Media.

◆ ◆ ◆

Made in the USA
Middletown, DE
02 March 2020